Extreme Sports

by David Orme

Ransom

WORCESTERSHIRE COUNTY COUNCIL		
617		
Bertrams		28.10.06
		£4.99
WS		

Trailblazers

Extreme Sports
by David Orme
Educational consultant: Helen Bird

Illustrated by Demitri Nezis

Published by Ransom Publishing Ltd.
Rose Cottage, Howe Hill, Watlington, Oxon. OX49 5HB
www.ransom.co.uk

ISBN   184167 590 3
        978 184167 590 9

First published in 2006

Extreme Sports

Contents

EXtreme Sports

Get the facts

What are extreme sports?

They might be   ▣   Jumping from high places

▣   Going very fast

▣   Doing clever stunts.

Are they safe?

Even playing ordinary sports can be risky.
But extreme sports can be very dangerous.

It is important to -

▣   Get proper training in the sport before you try it yourself.

▣   Use the proper equipment – and check it is working properly.

▣   Be sensible. Showing off can risk your life – and other people's.

Why do people take part?

People say life is boring
these days.

Extreme sport can
put risks and
thrills back into
people's lives.

Would you
like to . . .

☑ Jump off the top of
a high building?

☑ Go downhill at over 100
miles per hour on a board
with no brakes?

☑ Surf the world's biggest waves?

If you would, extreme sport may
be just the thing for you!

Sports on wheels

Dirt biking has a course with steep places, obstacles, and lots of mud.

Riders go round one at a time. The fastest rider wins.

Dirt biking is for powered and unpowered bikes.

Other extreme (and dangerous!) cycling sports are BMX, freestyle, downhill and jumps.

Skateboards were invented by surfers. They could practice on them when they couldn't get to the sea.

Skateboarding is one of the most popular sports, and the stunts are amazing!

Street luge is one of the scariest extreme sports.

Racers lie on a special skateboard. They race downhill at up to 100 mph, steering with their bodies. There are NO BRAKES!

9

Air sports

Paragliding uses a special parachute. The parachute fills with air as it moves forward. This keeps it rigid.

Paragliders run and jump off high places. They steer the paraglider by pulling on the ropes.

Some paragliders fix motors to their backs. This means that they can take off from the ground and control where they go.

Hang gliders are really small aeroplanes. The wings have a metal frame.

They take off from high places too.

Hang gliders can have motors.

These hang gliders are called **microlights**. They can take off and land like a normal plane.

A new extreme sport - **human powered aircraft.**

These very light aircraft have flown over 100 km. To fly one, you have to be super fit – and keep pedalling!

11

Jumping sports

Imagine standing on the top of a high crane. Then you jump off. (Or maybe someone pushes you if you are too scared.) The ground rushes up towards you.

The only thing that will save you is a rubber rope tied to your feet, and a harness.

But will it stop you in time?

This is **bungee jumping**!

Are you up for it?

Done that? Then try - bungee jumping from a HELICOPTER!

Skydiving

Skydivers jump from aircraft at around 12,000 feet. They fall at about 125 mph, and open their parachutes between 2,000 and 400 feet from the ground.

One skydiver said

"You can do everything a bird does apart from go back up."

Once you become a safe skydiver, why not try **skysurfing**?

BASE jumping

BASE jumpers jump from

Buildings

Aerials or antennae (such as TV masts)

Spans (meaning bridges) and

Earth (usually the top of high cliffs) - with a parachute.

BASE jumpers need to be experts with parachutes. There is no time to make mistakes!

Water sports

Surfing is popular wherever there are big waves. But when the waves get too big the surfing has to stop – but not for extreme surfers!

Some surfers say surfing in the middle of winter is extreme surfing. The waves might not be dangerous, but it is extremely cold!

This is kitesurfing. The kites pull you at up to 30 mph!

It is a dangerous sport. You can end up 5 metres up in the air – it hurts when you hit the water!

If you are not in control, the kite can drag you into boats or rocks.

White-water kayaks
are small, light boats
made of plastic.

Beginners are taught
to kayak in safe places.

Extreme kayakers choose
the most dangerous parts of the river.

If the water conditions are dangerous
they may be injured or killed.

Crazy sports

All extreme sports are dangerous. Some of them are crazy as well.

Cheese rolling sounds safe. But every year people get hurt taking part.

How it works: Someone throws a big cheese down a very steep hill, in Gloucestershire, England.

Lots of crazy people chase after it.

The winner is the person who gets the cheese first.

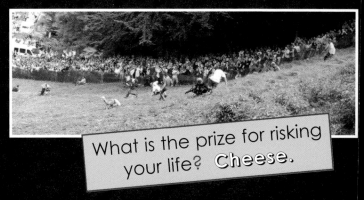

What is the prize for risking your life? Cheese.

Going over Niagara Falls in a barrel

The first crazy person to do this was Annie Taylor in 1901. She lived, but many people who have tried it have died.

Buildering

The most famous climber of buildings is Spiderman.

But some people do it for real!

Alan Robert is the most famous 'urban climber'.

He climbs high buildings without any safety gear. When he gets to the top, the cops are waiting for him!

Don't try this at home – *or anywhere else!*

The craziest sport of all – Extreme Ironing

Ironing at home is boring, so why not do it somewhere really dangerous?

- **Underwater ironing**
- **Freefall ironing**
- **Mountain ironing**
- **Tight-rope ironing**.

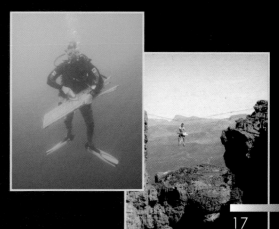

The
Climb

Chapter 1:
Trouble with parents

Rob hadn't wanted to come in the first place. He didn't want to sit on the beach making sandcastles. But Rob had two little sisters.

"It's their turn to choose the holiday," Dad had said.

Rob loved climbing in the hills. He had wanted to go somewhere where he could do that. But his parents said no.

"You went on that climbing camp in the spring," Mum said. "Now it's the girls' turn."

It was nearly the end of the holiday, and Rob was fed up. It had been a boring day sitting on the beach. His sisters had moaned all the time.

"Rob won't play with us!"

"Rob, don't just sit there. Play with your sisters!"

Rob snapped. He got up and stormed off.

Chapter 2:
Alone

There were tall cliffs nearby. Rob walked round some rocks and found he was in a small bay. No-one else was there. Great! He could be alone.

He walked and walked. It was getting late. The family would be packing up. Rob didn't care. He just walked.

Then he heard water splashing. The tide was coming in, fast. He looked back. He would never make it to the rocks in time!

The water was washing up over his feet. Rob knew there was only one thing for it.

He would have to climb the cliff.

Rob was a good climber, but to do it properly you need equipment. All Rob had were his bare hands.

Chapter 3:
Stuck

The bottom of the cliff was an easy climb. Lumps of flint stuck out of the rock. They gave him something to hang on to.

Rob looked up. It was a long, long way. He could see seagulls high in the sky. A pair of wings would come in really handy now.

He found a crack in the rock. Great. He could wedge himself in it and push himself up.

Slowly, he moved up the cliff. He was at least ten metres above the beach. One slip and he would fall and probably be killed. He looked down. The sea was well in now. He couldn't go back down.

He felt dizzy. Don't look down again!

Then he got to the top of the crack. He was stuck.

Chapter 4:
Carefully . . .

He looked up. He could see the top of the cliff about three metres above. But to get to it he would have to swing out of the crack and climb the bare rock, with only his fingers and toes to stop him falling.

He wiggled sideways. He got his foot onto a big flint and it held. He looked for a hand hold. There. A tiny crack!

He looked up. Another crack, just in reach. He pushed up with his feet. Got it. Now for another foothold. There! Bit of a stretch though. Carefully . . .

The foothold gave way. Rob was hanging by his fingers, and it was agony. His feet were flapping wildly. Calm down. Look. Another flint – Left foot this time. It held!

Push, push. A clump of grass to hang on to. It was the cliff top!

With a heave Rob scrambled over and lay panting on the ground.

There was a path along the cliff top. An old man was sitting on a bench. He was very surprised to see Rob.

"Where did you come from?"

But Rob was shaking too much to speak.

Extreme sports word check

building	parachute
climbing	pedalling
control	powered
course	practice
dangerous	rigid
downhill	risky
equipment	rubber
experts	rushes
gear	scariest
harness	sensible
imagine	steering
invented	stunts
ironing	surfers
kite	thrills
microlights	training
motors	unpowered
obstacles	urban climber
ordinary	winner